Earth Smart

FIRST EDITION
Series Editors Deborah Lock and Penny Smith; **US Editor** John Searcy; **Art Editor** Sonia Moore;
DTP Designer Almudena Díaz; **Production** Angela Graef; **Jacket Designer** Sonia Moore;
Photographer Andy Crawford; **Reading Consultant** Linda Gambrell, PhD

THIS EDITION
Editorial Management by Oriel Square
Produced for DK by WonderLab Group LLC
Jennifer Emmett, Erica Green, Kate Hale, *Founders*

Editors Grace Hill Smith, Libby Romero, Maya Myers, Michaela Weglinski;
Photography Editors Kelley Miller, Annette Kiesow, Nicole DiMella; **Managing Editor** Rachel Houghton;
Designers Project Design Company; **Researcher** Michelle Harris; **Copy Editor** Lori Merritt;
Indexer Connie Binder; **Proofreader** Larry Shea; **Reading Specialist** Dr. Jennifer Albro;
Curriculum Specialist Elaine Larson

Published in the United States by DK Publishing
1745 Broadway, 20th Floor, New York, NY 10019

Copyright © 2023 Dorling Kindersley Limited
DK, a Division of Penguin Random House LLC
22 23 24 25 26 10 9 8 7 6 5 4 3 2 1
001–334107–July/2023

A catalog record for this book
is available from the Library of Congress.
HC ISBN: 978-0-7440-7501-4
PB ISBN: 978-0-7440-7502-1

DK books are available at special discounts when purchased in bulk for sales promotions, premiums,
fundraising, or educational use. For details, contact: DK Publishing Special Markets,
1745 Broadway, 20th Floor, New York, NY 10019
SpecialSales@dk.com

Printed and bound in China

The publisher would like to thank the following for their kind permission to reproduce their images:
a=above; c=center; b=below; l=left; r=right; t=top; b/g=background

Dreamstime.com: Ingrid Balabanova 20br, Marcello Celli 9b, Iakov Filimonov 28b, Anahit Gevorgyan 21t, Paul Glover 13br,
Vlad Ispas 22–23, Dmitry Kuznetsov 14b, Photka 14c, 15bl, 16b, Sburel 26b, Aekkarak Thongjiew 20cl, Dong Tian 24–25t,
Angelina Zinovieva 16–17t; **Getty Images / iStock:** mphillips007 1bc, Marilyn Nieves 27br, Michele Pevide 7;
Shutterstock.com: Ray Morgan 8c

Cover images: *Front:* **Shutterstock.com:** A3pfamily, IrDesign90 b; *Back:* **Shutterstock.com:** MarcoVector clb, photka cra

All other images © Dorling Kindersley
For more information see: www.dkimages.com

For the curious
www.dk.com

Earth Smart

Leslie Garrett

Contents

Caring for the Environment

"Hooray!" shouted Spencer.

"Aunt Charlotte brought us ice pops!"

Aunt Charlotte was looking after Spencer and his older sister, Sophie, for the day.

Aunt Charlotte is a teacher. Her classes are about the environment—the world around us.

"We can all take good care of the environment," she told the children.

Yum!

Aunt Charlotte gave Sophie and Spencer their ice pops.

Spencer tore off the wrapper and tossed it on the ground.

Put a Lid on It

Keep your environment clean by putting trash in a garbage can or taking it home. Keep a lid on your can at home so garbage doesn't blow away.

Sophie bent down to pick it up. "We shouldn't litter," she said.

She dropped the wrapper and her napkin into a nearby garbage can.

Aunt Charlotte agreed: "We need to keep our planet clean so it's a healthy place to live."

Off to the Landfill

Just then a garbage truck stopped at the curb.

A man emptied the garbage can into the back of the truck.

Landfill Site

Garbage is spread out and covered with earth to keep flies away and cut down on smell.

"Where is he taking the garbage?" asked Spencer.

"It goes to a landfill," said Aunt Charlotte.

"That's a huge pit in the ground where garbage is dumped, then covered over with earth. After a long time, some of the garbage breaks down and becomes dirt."

"We should be careful about the garbage we throw out," said Aunt Charlotte.

"Some things are toxic."

"What's toxic?" asked Spencer.

"Things like cans of paint and batteries leak out dangerous chemicals that can get into our soil and water," replied Aunt Charlotte.

leaking batteries

"If you have dangerous trash like this, get adults to take it to a hazardous waste drop-off center, where it will be disposed of safely."

Batteries

You will throw away fewer batteries if you use rechargeable batteries or windup radios and flashlights.

Recycling Waste

The children followed Aunt Charlotte into the house.

"We throw away too much," Aunt Charlotte continued.

"We should recycle as much as we can. That means saving things like glass bottles, plastic food wrappers, and cans, so they can be reused or melted down and turned into something else."

a vase made from recycled glass

Recycling Cans

Aluminum cans can be recycled over and over again. The metal always stays strong and flexible.

"Let's set up recycling boxes," said Sophie.

She found three big boxes and stuck labels on them that said "paper," "plastic," and "glass and cans."

Spencer found some old newspapers his mother was going to throw away.
He put them in the "paper" recycling box.

Recycling Bins

If your recycling boxes are not collected, you can empty them into recycling bins at a local drop-off point.

Reducing Air Pollution

"Another way to help our planet is to save electricity," said Aunt Charlotte.

"Power plants burn fuel to make electricity," she said.

"Smoke from the burning fuel makes the air dirty." Spencer coughed.

"We breathe the pollution," he said.

"Without clean air, we get sick," said Sophie.

Aunt Charlotte nodded. "And so can our planet," she said.

"The pollution in the air traps heat and makes the planet heat up," explained Aunt Charlotte.

"This is called global warming. Ice is melting at both the North and South Poles. This means there will be more floods, and people and animals will lose their homes."

Melting Snow

Global warming is making snow melt on Africa's tallest mountain, Mount Kilimanjaro.

"If we use less electricity, we will make less pollution," said Aunt Charlotte.

"Do you know how we can use less at home?" she asked.

"We can turn off lights when we don't need them," suggested Spencer, as he turned off a light.

"We can read books instead of watching TV," added Sophie.

The TV was on, so Sophie turned it off.

Earth-Smart Living

Later, they all went to the park.

"Phew," said Spencer as they walked beside a busy road.

"What's that smell?"

"That's exhaust from the car engines," said Aunt Charlotte.

"It pollutes the air."

"If we walk, we'll cut down on pollution," Sophie suggested.

Aunt Charlotte nodded.

They arrived at the park and found a place to have a picnic.

"I like the plants and trees in the park," said Sophie.

"Trees protect us from air pollution," said Aunt Charlotte.

"They give off oxygen, which we can breathe. Trees and other plants make the air healthier. They also provide homes for many kinds of animals."

They opened
a bag of strawberries.

"These are from your uncle's
farm," Aunt Charlotte said.

"He grows them organically.
That means he doesn't use
chemicals that can harm
the environment."

"Is that why they're so sweet?" asked Spencer.

"Probably," laughed Aunt Charlotte.

"He sells them at the local farmer's market. Since he doesn't travel far, he doesn't create much pollution."

On the way home, Aunt Charlotte and the children stopped at the grocery store.

They had to buy food for dinner. They checked the labels to find food grown as close as possible to their town.

They found beans, squash, and chicken, with yogurt for dessert.

As they went home, Sophie said, "Thanks for teaching us to take care of the planet, Aunt Charlotte. Now, we can help cut down on pollution."

"And recycle," her aunt added.

Spencer picked a chewing-gum wrapper off the ground.

"And I won't litter!" he said.

Glossary

Environment
Everything in an area, including the land, climate, and living things

Exhaust
The smoke or gas given off by an engine

Global warming
An increase in the world's temperatures

Landfill
A huge pit in the ground where garbage is dumped and covered with soil

Litter
To scatter waste on the ground

Organic
Produced naturally, without chemicals

Oxygen
A gas in the air that we breathe

Pollution
Poisons and other materials that are dirty or harmful

Recycle
To use things again

Toxic
Poisonous

Index

Quiz

Answer the questions to see what you have learned. Check your answers in the key below.

1. What happens to garbage after it goes to a landfill?

2. Why are paint and batteries considered to be dangerous trash?

3. What causes global warming?

4. How do trees protect us from air pollution?

5. What kind of crops are grown without using chemicals?

 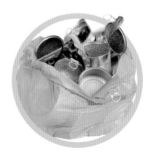 

1. It breaks down and becomes dirt 2. They leak out chemicals that get into soil and water 3. Pollution in the air traps heat
4. They give off oxygen, which we can breathe 5. Organic